A KID'S GUIDE TO FEELINGS

FEELING SAD

BY KIRSTY HOLMES

KidHaven
PUBLISHING

Published in 2019 by KidHaven Publishing, an Imprint of Greenhaven Publishing, LLC
353 3rd Avenue, Suite 255, New York, NY 10010

This edition is published by arrangement with Booklife Publishing.

Written by: Kirsty Holmes
Edited by: John Wood
Designed by: Danielle Rippengill

Cataloging-in-Publication Data

Names: Holmes, Kirsty.
Title: Feeling sad / Kirsty Holmes.
Description: New York : KidHaven Publishing, 2019. | Series: A kid's guide to feelings | Includes glossary and index.
Identifiers: ISBN 9781534526761 (pbk.) | ISBN 9781534526754 (library bound) | ISBN 9781534526778 (6 pack)
Subjects: LCSH: Sadness in children--Juvenile literature. | Emotions--Juvenile literature.
Classification: LCC BF723.S15 H645 2019 | DDC 155.4'124--dc23

Image Credits: All images are courtesy of Shutterstock.com, unless otherwise specified.
With thanks to Getty Images, Thinkstock Photo and iStockphoto. Front Cover – MarinaMay,
yayasya, jirawat phueksriphan, Piotr Urakau, Andrea Slatter, Halfbottle, ViChizh.
Images used on every page – MarinaMay, yayasya, Piotr Urakau. 5 & 6 – Oxy_gen,
Ksusha Dusmikeeva, kondratya. 8 – PHILIPIMAGE, wavebreakmedia, Paul Biryukov.
9 – tkhatsko, Santhosh Varghese, LightField Studios, Luca Santilli. 11 – wavebreakmedia,
all_about_people, Firma V, AlenD. 12 – raysay, Halfbottle, Evellean. 13 – Evellean, medesulda,
Yuliia Oliinyk. 14 – vladwel, Musaffar Patel, Succo Design. 15 – Africa Studio, krutar, Svitlana–ua.
16 – Veronica Louro. 17 – iko. 18 – STUDIO GRAND OUEST. 21 – Mama Belle Love kids, Yiorgos
GR. 21, 22 & 23 – Oxy_gen, Ksusha Dusmikeeva, kondratya.

Printed in the United States of America

CPSIA compliance information: Batch # BS18KL: For further information contact Greenhaven Publishing LLC, New York, New York at 1-844-317-7404.

CONTENTS

Words that look like **this** can be found in the glossary on page 24.

We all have **emotions**, or feelings, all the time. Our feelings are very important. They help us think about the world around us, and know how we want to **react**.

Sometimes, we feel good. Other times, we feel bad.

It looks like it's the end for Dr. Gloom's ice cream! Dr. Gloom is feeling really sad.

Let's find out more…

HOW DO WE FEEL WHEN WE'RE SAD?

You might have a **sinking** feeling in your belly…

…you might feel a lump in your throat…

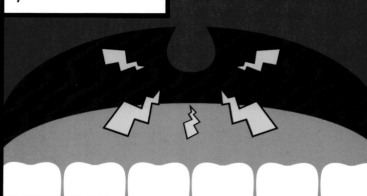

…you might feel an **ache** in your chest…

… or you might feel tears in your eyes.

8

HOW DO WE LOOK WHEN WE'RE SAD?

THINGS THAT MAKE US SAD

WHEN FEELING SAD IS GOOD

Feeling sad can help us. Sadness tells us that something is not OK. This means we can try to change it.

When we cry, or look sad, people will come and help us. They can give us a hug, or help us **solve** our problem.

It is nice to be looked after.

WHEN FEELING SAD IS BAD

It's OK to feel sad when something happens you don't like…

SAD FEELINGS SHOULDN'T LAST TOO LONG.

…but people don't usually feel sad all the time.

If you are sad all the time, tell someone you **trust**. 19

DEALING WITH FEELINGS

Dr. Gloom needs to feel looked after.

His friends will help him to feel better. Agents of F.E.E.L.S: GO!

LET'S HELP!

Talking about your feelings can help you to understand why you feel sad.

It's OK to cry…

YOU'RE CRYING.

WE CAN SHARE MINE.

I FEEL BETTER NOW. THANK YOU.

THE END

23

GLOSSARY

ACHE	hurt with a dull, constant pain
BODY LANGUAGE	things a person does with their body that tell you how they feel
EMOTIONS	a strong feeling such as joy, hate, sadness, or fear
REACT	act or respond to something that has happened or been done
SINKING	a heavy or dropping feeling
SOCIETY	a collection of people living together in a group
SOLVE	to find or figure out an answer to a problem
TREMBLING	shaking movements
TRUST	believe that someone is good, reliable, and tells the truth

INDEX